AF316685

THE ETHICAL EDUCATOR

PRINCIPLES FOR TEACHING AND LEARNING

DR. MINAKSHI BANSAL

Dedicated to educators everywhere—

those tireless guardians of learning who ignite curiosity and foster an environment where integrity and compassion illuminate the path of every student.

And to my mentors, whose guidance and unwavering support have shaped my journey more profoundly than words can express.

ᗘᗘᗘ

Contents

Contents

Prayer

"Om Bhadram Karnebhih Shrinuyama Devah
Bhadram Pashyemakshabhiryajatrah
Sthirairangais Tushtuvamsastanubhih
Vyashema Devahitam Yadayuh
Svasti Na Indro Vriddhashravah
Svasti Nah Pusha Vishwavedah
Svasti Nastarkshyo Arishtanemih
Svasti No Brihaspatir Dadhatu
Om Shantih Shantih Shantih"

This mantra is a prayer for universal well-being, invoking the blessings of various deities for protection, health, and happiness. It emphasizes the importance of experiencing the auspicious through all senses and living a life aligned with divine purpose. The repetition of "Shantih" at the end signifies a deep desire for peace in the individual, the environment, and the universe at large. This mantra is often recited as a prayer for peace, prosperity, and the physical and spiritual well-being of all beings.

❧❧❧

Preface

Education is one of the most profound endeavors that individuals and societies undertake, molding the minds and values of generations and, by extension, shaping the future of communities and nations. At the heart of this complex, transformative process are educators—those entrusted not only with the transmission of knowledge but also with the responsibility of nurturing ethical, thoughtful, and responsible individuals. The role of an educator extends far beyond imparting academic skills; it involves modeling values, making ethical decisions, and cultivating an environment where ethical considerations are as integral as the curriculum itself.

In this book, we delve into the various dimensions of ethics in education. We explore the foundational role that ethics plays in the teaching profession and the critical importance of educators developing and maintaining their ethical compass. This is not merely about adhering to professional codes of conduct; it is about embracing the deeper moral responsibilities that come with the profound influence educators have on their students. By fostering environments of fairness, respect, and integrity, educators do more than teach; they inspire and transform.

Ethical challenges in education are multifaceted. They range from ensuring fairness and inclusion in the classroom to handling personal and institutional biases, all the way to integrating technology in ways that honor both educational goals and students' privacy. Each of these challenges demands careful thought, deliberate action, and a steadfast commitment to what is just and right. This book provides educators with the tools and perspectives necessary to navigate these complex issues. Through a combination of theoretical insights and practical advice, it aims to guide educators in becoming exemplary models of ethical behavior and decision-making.

Reflective practice is another cornerstone of ethical teaching explored in this book. The ability to reflect critically on one's actions and decisions is invaluable, not only in honing one's teaching practice but also in evaluating the ethical implications of these actions. Reflection enables educators to consider not just the effectiveness of their teaching methods but also the impact of their ethical choices on students' learning and development. It encourages educators to ask not just whether they are teaching well, but whether they are doing good.

Moreover, the book addresses the broader implications of ethical teaching and learning. It considers how educators can foster ethical awareness and critical thinking in their students, thereby contributing to the development of morally conscious individuals. This is particularly crucial in today's globalized world, where students will face complex social, environmental, and ethical challenges. Educators have the unique opportunity to equip students with not only the knowledge but also the ethical discernment to tackle these issues responsibly.

In exploring these themes, the book draws upon a range of philosophical, educational, and psychological perspectives, providing a rich and diverse exploration of what it means to be an ethical educator. It also incorporates case studies and real-life examples, illustrating how ethical dilemmas manifest in educational settings and how they can be addressed. These examples serve as practical illustrations of the abstract principles discussed, grounding them in the everyday realities of teaching.

Furthermore, the book examines the institutional context within which educators operate. It recognizes that ethical teaching is not just about individual educators but also about the educational systems within which they work. Therefore, it discusses how educational policies and leadership can either support or hinder the ethical commitments of educators. It advocates for policies that uphold ethical standards and promote a culture of integrity throughout educational institutions.

Lastly, this book is an invitation—a call to educators to continually strive for ethical excellence. It acknowledges that the journey of an ethical educator is one of ongoing learning and growth. There are no final answers or perfect solutions in the realm of ethics. Instead, there are principles to guide, dilemmas to navigate, and continuous opportunities for reflection and improvement.

As readers engage with the content of this book, it is hoped that they find both inspiration and practical guidance. The aim is not only to inform but also to empower educators to act ethically and confidently, knowing that their choices shape not only the minds but also the characters of those they teach. In fostering ethical awareness and practice, educators contribute to a more just, thoughtful, and compassionate world. This book is dedicated to all such educators who commit themselves to this noble and essential pursuit.

Dr. Minakshi Bansal
Social Activist
Ahmedabad, Gujarat, Bharat

◁◁◁

About The Author

Dr. Minakshi Bansal, born in the bustling metropolis of Delhi, India, has led a life steeped in artistry, scholarly pursuit, and an unwavering commitment to societal betterment. Following her marriage, she relocated to Ahmedabad, Gujarat, where she has since blossomed into a multifaceted beacon of inspiration for many. Dr. Minakshi is not only recognized as a gifted artist in the realm of Fine Arts but also as an esteemed author, a devoted social worker and a dedicated research scholar in Psychology. Her journey, marked by a profound dedication to elevating those around her, especially the downtrodden and underprivileged children of society, is a testament to her deep-seated belief in the transformative power of engagement and empathy.

From her earliest days, Minakshi was distinguished by an insatiable appetite for reading. Her literary universe was inhabited by characters and narratives that spanned ethical tales, motivational and inspirational stories, and the mythic parables imbued with life lessons. This voracious reading habit was not merely for personal edification but was driven by a desire to distill and disseminate the essence of these narratives to foster the development of students and peers alike. She was particularly captivated by the lives and teachings of historical figures and spiritual leaders such as Adi Shankaracharya, Swami Vivekananda, Dr. APJ Abdul Kalam, Mahamana Pandit Madan Mohan Malviya, Mahatma Gandhi, Sardar Vallabhai Patel, and Vinoba Bhave, among others. Their philosophies and life stories fueled her ambition to embody their ideals of resilience, selflessness, and relentless pursuit of knowledge.

Dr. Minakshi's academic and practical engagement with psychology has been equally noteworthy. As a research scholar, her focus has been on exploring the intricate tapestry of the human psyche, aiming to unlock the potential for psychological well-being and societal harmony. Her scholarly work is complemented by her active involvement in social work, where she employs her academic insights to make tangible differences in the lives of the underprivileged. Her endeavours in social work are characterized by an innovative approach that combines traditional wisdom with contemporary psychological practices to address the multifaceted challenges faced by these communities.

Her artistic talents, another facet of her diverse capabilities, are not merely a personal passion but also serve as a medium through which she communicates and connects with others. Her art, rich in symbolism and emotional depth, reflects her philosophical inquiries and social concerns, offering viewers a glimpse into the breadth of her intellect and the depth of her compassion.

In addition to her contributions to the arts and social sciences, Dr. Minakshi has embraced the healing arts of Pranic Healing, mastering the techniques developed by Master Choa Kok Sui. This practice, which focuses on the manipulation of Prana or life energy to heal the body and aura, has been both a personal journey of discovery and a means through which she extends her healing touch to others. Her proficiency in Pranic Healing is complemented by her advocacy and teaching of various forms of meditation aimed at rejuvenation, personal betterment, and the cultivation of harmony within individuals and communities alike.

Dr. Minakshi's life is a narrative of relentless pursuit, not just of personal achievement but of the upliftment and empowerment of society at large. Her diverse interests and talents—spanning the arts, literature, psychology, and the healing practices—converge on a singular path of service. She embodies the spirit of the luminaries who inspired her, channelling their legacy through her actions and teachings. Through her books, art, and social initiatives, she continues to inspire a new generation to embark on their own journeys of self-discovery, resilience, and altruism.

Her commitment to social betterment, particularly her focus on uplifting underprivileged children, reflects a deep understanding of the transformative potential of education and personal development. By integrating her knowledge of psychology, her artistic sensibilities, and her healing practices, Dr. Bansal has developed a holistic approach to social work that addresses both the immediate needs and the long-term well-being of the communities she serves.

As an author, Dr. Minakshi's writings offer a blend of inspirational insights, practical wisdom, and reflective contemplations drawn from her extensive reading and life experiences. Her books serve as a guide for those seeking to navigate the complexities of life with grace, resilience, and purpose. Through her narratives, she extends an invitation to her readers to explore the depths of their own potential and to contribute meaningfully to the collective well-being of society.

In Dr. Minakshi Bansal, we find a remarkable synthesis of the artist, the scholar, the healer, and the social activist. Her life's work stands as a beacon of hope and a source of inspiration for individuals seeking to make a difference in the world. Her story is a compelling reminder of the power of individual action, rooted in compassion and driven by a profound commitment to the betterment of humanity. Dr. Minakshi's legacy is not just in the tangible outcomes of her efforts but in the enduring spirit of inquiry, empathy, and service that she embodies.

ᐅᐅᐅ

ONE

THE FOUNDATIONS OF ETHICAL EDUCATION

Ethical education begins with an understanding of the core values that are essential to fostering an environment of integrity, fairness, and respect in any learning setting. These core values serve as the bedrock for all teaching practices and interactions within the educational sphere. It is crucial for educators to establish a strong ethical foundation to not only guide their own behaviors but also to set a positive example for students.

Core Values of Ethical Education

At the heart of ethical education lies a commitment to values such as honesty, respect, fairness, responsibility, and compassion. Each of these values plays a pivotal role in shaping the moral framework within which students learn and interact. For instance, honesty in the classroom translates to transparent communication between teachers and students, fostering a trust-based relationship that is conducive to learning. Respect involves acknowledging the inherent worth and dignity of each individual, regardless of their background or beliefs, which helps in creating an inclusive and supportive educational environment.

Fairness is another critical element, ensuring that all students are given equal opportunities to succeed and that judgments are made impartially and based on merit. Responsibility in education involves both teachers and students taking accountability for their actions and their learning, promoting a sense of ownership and commitment to educational goals. Lastly, compassion encourages empathy and understanding, qualities that are essential for addressing the personal and academic challenges that students may face.

Implementing Ethical Practices

Implementing these core values requires specific strategies and practices that embed ethics into the daily routines and overarching policies of educational institutions. One effective approach is the development and consistent enforcement of a code of ethics. This code should clearly outline the expectations for behavior from all members of the educational community, including staff, students, and administrators. It acts as a guideline for appropriate conduct and a reference point in resolving ethical dilemmas.

Another important practice is the integration of ethics into the curriculum. Educators can incorporate discussions of moral dilemmas, ethical decision-making, and the consequences of unethical behavior into their lessons, regardless of the subject matter. This not only enhances students' understanding of ethics but also helps them apply ethical considerations to various aspects of life.

Role of Leadership in Ethical Education

Leadership plays a critical role in establishing and maintaining the ethical standards of an educational institution. Leaders must exemplify the ethical behaviors they expect to see in their staff and students, creating a culture where ethical practices are valued and promoted. This involves providing ongoing training and support for educators in ethical decision-making and problem-solving.

Moreover, ethical leadership involves openness to feedback and a willingness to address ethical issues as they arise. By maintaining open lines of communication and fostering a culture of honesty and accountability, educational leaders can ensure that ethical breaches are handled promptly and effectively.

Ethical Challenges and Solutions

Despite the best efforts to establish a solid ethical foundation, challenges such as discrimination, inequality, and unethical behavior can still arise. Addressing these challenges requires a proactive approach, including monitoring for ethical compliance and implementing corrective measures when necessary. Regular ethical audits and assessments can help identify areas where the institution may be falling short of its ethical commitments.

Additionally, creating a safe and confidential way for students and staff to report unethical behavior is crucial in maintaining ethical standards. This not only helps in early detection of issues but also reinforces the institution's commitment to upholding ethical values.

The foundations of ethical education are built on a commitment to core values that foster respect, fairness, and integrity within the educational environment. By implementing strong ethical practices, providing leadership that embodies these values, and addressing challenges proactively, educational institutions can create a nurturing and morally sound environment that is conducive to learning and personal development. This foundational approach not only benefits the students academically and personally but also prepares them to engage ethically in broader societal contexts.

ᚦᚦᚦ

"True education extends beyond imparting knowledge; it involves molding character, instilling the courage to act with integrity in the face of challenges."

▷▷▷

TWO
Cultivating Integrity in the Classroom

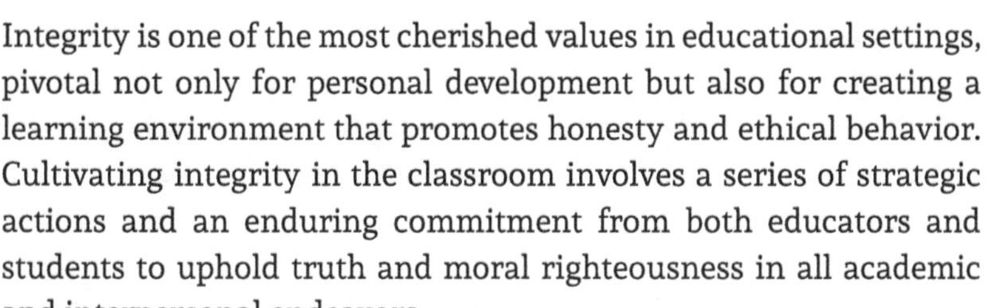

Integrity is one of the most cherished values in educational settings, pivotal not only for personal development but also for creating a learning environment that promotes honesty and ethical behavior. Cultivating integrity in the classroom involves a series of strategic actions and an enduring commitment from both educators and students to uphold truth and moral righteousness in all academic and interpersonal endeavors.

Establishing a Culture of Honesty

To foster integrity, educators must first establish a culture of honesty. This involves setting clear expectations for students about the importance of honesty in all their actions, including homework, examinations, and in their interactions with peers and teachers. Educators themselves must model these behaviors, demonstrating the value of honesty in everyday situations. For example, when grading, teachers should provide fair, consistent feedback that reflects the student's actual performance, and in discussions, they should acknowledge any lack of knowledge and commit to providing accurate information.

Promoting Academic Honesty

Academic honesty is a critical aspect of integrity in education. Teachers need to explicitly teach students what constitutes cheating and plagiarism and why these practices are harmful not just to their learning but to the trust built within the classroom community. Implementing honor codes or integrity contracts can be effective in making expectations explicit. These documents require students to pledge their commitment to uphold the school's standards of honesty, which can have a powerful psychological impact on their behavior.

Engaging students in discussions about the consequences of dishonesty and the benefits of academic integrity helps them understand the broader implications of their actions. By discussing real-world examples of academic dishonesty and its impact on individuals and institutions, students can better appreciate the importance of integrity in both their academic and future professional lives.

Encouraging Personal Responsibility

Personal responsibility is inherently linked to integrity. Students should be encouraged to take responsibility for their actions and their learning. This can be facilitated by creating a learning environment where students set their own academic goals and assess their progress towards these goals. Such practices empower students and foster a sense of ownership over their learning process, reducing the temptation to engage in dishonest behavior.

Teachers can further this by implementing reflective practices that prompt students to evaluate their own work and decision-making processes. Reflection journals, for example, can be a practical tool for students to record their challenges, successes, and ethical dilemmas, allowing them to think critically about their own behavior and choices.

Building Trust Through Transparency

Transparency in teaching methods and assessment criteria also plays a crucial role in cultivating integrity. When students understand how their work is evaluated and what the criteria are, they are more likely to see the assessment as fair and are less inclined to cheat. Furthermore, being transparent about classroom rules and the rationale behind them can help students feel respected and understood, which enhances their trust in the system and encourages them to adhere to its rules.

Encouraging a Supportive Classroom Environment

A supportive classroom environment where students feel valued and respected is essential for promoting integrity. This environment is characterized by open communication, where students feel safe to express their ideas and concerns without fear of ridicule or retribution. Establishing regular check-ins and fostering a classroom culture where students support each other can discourage behaviors that compromise integrity, such as bullying or cheating.

Role of Feedback and Recognition

Providing constructive feedback and recognizing students when they display integrity are also effective strategies. Positive reinforcement can reinforce the desired behaviors and serve as a powerful motivator for other students. Celebrating acts of honesty and integrity, such as returning lost items or admitting a mistake, can help reinforce these values as part of the classroom's culture.

Cultivating integrity in the classroom requires consistent efforts to promote honesty, responsibility, and trust. By establishing clear expectations, engaging students in discussions about ethics, and creating a supportive learning environment, educators can instill a strong sense of integrity in their students. This foundation not only enhances the educational experience but also prepares students to lead ethical lives outside the classroom.

꒰꒰꒰

"The heart of teaching lies not just in the content delivered but in the values demonstrated through every interaction in the classroom."

ᔕᔕᔕ

THREE
Equity and Inclusion: Ensuring Fairness in Education

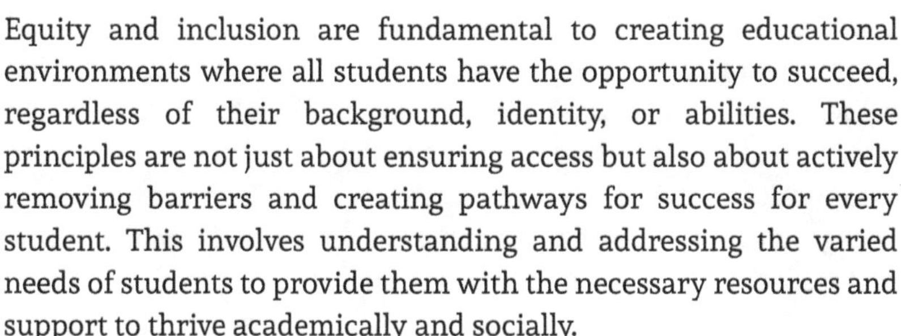

Equity and inclusion are fundamental to creating educational environments where all students have the opportunity to succeed, regardless of their background, identity, or abilities. These principles are not just about ensuring access but also about actively removing barriers and creating pathways for success for every student. This involves understanding and addressing the varied needs of students to provide them with the necessary resources and support to thrive academically and socially.

Understanding Equity versus Equality

To foster equity and inclusion, it is important to first distinguish between equity and equality. Equality involves treating everyone the same, often ignoring the disparate needs and circumstances of students. Equity, on the other hand, entails recognizing these differences and providing resources and opportunities tailored to meet individual needs. This approach ensures that all students have a fair chance to succeed, which might mean allocating more resources to those who are at a disadvantage.

Culturally Responsive Teaching

Culturally responsive teaching is a powerful approach to foster inclusion and equity in the classroom. This method involves recognizing and respecting the cultural backgrounds of students and integrating these perspectives into the curriculum and teaching practices. It encourages students to relate course content to their own cultural contexts, which enhances engagement and learning. Teachers can implement culturally responsive teaching by including diverse cultural materials in their lessons, recognizing and addressing cultural biases in existing curricula, and employing teaching methods that are inclusive of various learning styles.

Creating Inclusive Classrooms

Creating an inclusive classroom goes beyond curriculum and teaching strategies; it involves building a classroom culture that values diversity and promotes respect among students. This can be achieved by setting clear norms about respectful behavior and communication. Activities that encourage students to share their backgrounds and experiences can enhance mutual understanding and respect, reducing stereotypes and biases.

In addition, accessibility is a key component of inclusion. Ensuring that physical spaces, resources, and teaching methods are accessible to all students, including those with disabilities, is crucial. This may involve providing materials in various formats, using assistive technologies, and designing classroom layouts that accommodate all students.

Addressing Systemic Barriers

Equity in education also requires addressing systemic barriers that hinder the success of certain groups of students. This can include policies and practices that disproportionately affect students based on race, socioeconomic status, gender, or other characteristics. Schools and educators need to examine their policies and practices critically to identify and dismantle such barriers. This might involve revising disciplinary procedures, admissions policies, and grading systems to ensure they are fair and inclusive.

Support Systems and Resources

Providing adequate support systems and resources is critical for promoting equity. This includes academic support, such as tutoring and mentoring programs, and social-emotional support through counseling and extracurricular activities. Schools should ensure that these supports are accessible to all students, particularly those who are marginalized or at risk of falling behind.

Training and Professional Development

Ongoing training and professional development are essential for educators to effectively promote equity and inclusion. Training programs should cover topics such as cultural competence, anti-bias education, and strategies for creating inclusive classrooms. These programs not only equip teachers with the necessary skills but also help them reflect on their own biases and improve their teaching practices.

Community and Family Engagement

Engaging families and the community in education can also enhance equity. When schools build strong partnerships with families, they can better understand and address the challenges that students face outside of school. Community resources can supplement school efforts, providing students with additional support and opportunities. Schools can foster this engagement through regular communication, community events, and involving families in decision-making processes.

Ensuring fairness in education through equity and inclusion requires a multifaceted approach. It involves understanding the unique challenges and needs of all students, embedding culturally responsive practices in teaching, creating inclusive classroom environments, addressing systemic barriers, providing robust support systems, and engaging with families and the community. By committing to these principles, educators can build a more equitable educational system that fosters the success and well-being of every student.

ᐅᐅᐅ

"Equity in education means more than equal access; it demands that every student has the support they need to succeed in their own unique way."

❧❧❧

FOUR

TRANSPARENCY IN TEACHING METHODS

Transparency in teaching methods is crucial for fostering a trusting and effective educational environment. When educators are open about their teaching strategies, assessment criteria, and expectations, students are better equipped to understand the learning process and the rationale behind instructional decisions. This transparency not only enhances student engagement and accountability but also builds a collaborative atmosphere in the classroom where students feel valued and understood.

Clarifying Learning Objectives and Outcomes

The foundation of transparency in education is the clear articulation of learning objectives and outcomes. Educators must communicate what students are expected to learn and how this learning will be measured. This involves detailing the skills, knowledge, and attitudes students are expected to acquire by the end of a course or unit. By understanding these objectives, students can better focus their efforts and align their study strategies to meet these goals.

Transparent Assessment Practices

Assessment is a critical area where transparency is essential. Teachers should provide students with clear, understandable criteria for how their work will be evaluated. This includes detailed rubrics, examples of successful work, and thorough explanations of grading scales. Transparent assessment practices help demystify the grading process, reduce anxiety about evaluations, and encourage students to approach their assignments with a clear sense of direction.

In addition to explaining how assessments will be conducted, it is important for educators to offer feedback that is both informative and constructive. Feedback should not only highlight areas of improvement but should also commend strengths, providing specific advice on how to enhance learning and performance. This kind of feedback fosters a growth mindset among students, encouraging them to view challenges as opportunities for development.

Open Communication Channels

Maintaining open lines of communication is another pillar of transparency in teaching. Educators should be approachable and available to discuss students' concerns and questions regarding the course material, teaching methods, and assessments. Regular office hours, responsive communication via emails or learning management systems, and open discussions during class can help maintain a transparent and inclusive educational environment.

Furthermore, soliciting feedback from students about the course and teaching methods is a valuable practice. This can be achieved through informal check-ins or structured surveys. Listening to student feedback not only aids in adjusting teaching methods to better meet their needs but also shows students that their opinions are valued and considered in shaping their educational experience.

Involving Students in the Learning Process

Transparency extends into involving students in the learning process itself. This can be facilitated by engaging students in decision-making related to the course. Options like allowing students to choose topics for projects or papers, select which assignments to complete from a list of possibilities, or even propose modifications to the syllabus can enhance their investment and participation in the course.

Involvement also means being transparent about the limitations and challenges of certain teaching methods. Educators should discuss why they choose specific approaches and be open to exploring alternatives if those methods are not meeting students' learning needs. This collaborative approach can lead to more effective and tailored educational experiences.

Utilizing Technology to Enhance Transparency

Technology can play a significant role in enhancing transparency in teaching. Digital tools and learning management systems (LMS) can be used to provide students with easy access to course materials, assignments, grades, and feedback in real-time. These platforms can serve as a central hub for information, reducing misunderstandings and ensuring that all students have access to the resources they need to succeed.

Moreover, technology can facilitate more dynamic interactions between students and teachers. For example, forums and discussion boards allow for ongoing dialogue outside of classroom hours, providing a platform for clarifying doubts and deepening understanding.

Continuous Improvement and Professional Development

For educators, commitment to transparency should also involve continuous improvement of their own teaching practices. Engaging in professional development activities, staying updated with educational research, and reflecting on personal teaching experiences are crucial for maintaining effective and transparent methods. Sharing these insights and changes with students not only demonstrates a dedication to high-quality teaching but also models the importance of lifelong learning and adaptability.

Transparency in teaching methods is fundamental to creating an educational environment that promotes understanding, trust, and active engagement. By clearly communicating objectives, involving students in the learning process, maintaining open channels of communication, and continuously refining teaching practices, educators can significantly enhance the learning experience and outcomes for all students.

ppp

"Technology in the classroom brings infinite possibilities but also ethical responsibilities—to use it in ways that enhance rather than impede learning."

❦❦❦

FIVE

Respect and Dignity in Educational Settings

Respect and dignity form the cornerstone of any positive educational environment. Upholding these values within schools and classrooms is essential not only for fostering a sense of safety and belonging among students but also for promoting effective learning. When students and educators treat each other with respect and dignity, it creates a supportive and encouraging atmosphere that enhances educational outcomes.

Cultivating Mutual Respect

The cultivation of mutual respect in educational settings begins with the acknowledgment of the inherent worth of every individual in the classroom. Educators must lead by example, treating all students with fairness and consideration, regardless of their background, abilities, or performance. This approach sets a standard for students, guiding them in how to interact respectfully with their peers and teachers.

Respect in the classroom also extends to listening actively to others' viewpoints, valuing diverse opinions, and engaging in constructive dialogues. Teachers can foster this by creating opportunities for students to express themselves and by actively facilitating discussions where multiple perspectives are heard and valued. Such practices not only teach students how to respect differing viewpoints but also enrich the learning experience by exposing them to a broader range of ideas and understandings.

Promoting Dignity Through Inclusive Practices

Dignity in education is closely tied to inclusivity. Ensuring that every student feels respected and valued involves recognizing and addressing the unique challenges and needs they may face. This includes adapting teaching methods to accommodate different learning styles and abilities, and ensuring that all students have access to the resources they need to succeed.

Inclusive practices also involve being mindful of language and behaviors that could undermine the dignity of any student. Educators need to be aware of and actively counteract biases, stereotypes, or discriminatory practices that may exist within the classroom. This might involve revising curriculum materials to include a wider range of cultural perspectives, or adjusting classroom policies to be more equitable.

Establishing a Safe and Supportive Environment

A safe and supportive learning environment is vital for upholding respect and dignity. This involves not only physical safety but also emotional and psychological safety. Schools should have clear policies and procedures in place to deal with bullying, harassment, and any form of abuse. These policies must be communicated clearly to all members of the school community and implemented consistently to protect the well-being of students.

Educators can further enhance a supportive atmosphere by being accessible and approachable, making themselves available to students who need help or advice. Additionally, fostering a classroom environment where mistakes are viewed as learning opportunities rather than failures can significantly enhance students' self-respect and encourage them to take intellectual risks.

Encouraging Empathy and Understanding

Teaching empathy and fostering an understanding of diverse life experiences are essential for nurturing respect and dignity. Through curriculum choices that expose students to different cultures, histories, and narratives, educators can help students develop a deeper understanding of the world around them and the varied experiences of people within it.

Classroom activities that encourage students to step into others' shoes, such as role-playing exercises or collaborative projects involving community engagement, can also be effective. These activities not only build empathy but also teach students the practical skills needed to navigate and respect cultural and individual differences.

Role of Leadership in Promoting Respect and Dignity

Leadership in educational settings plays a crucial role in establishing and maintaining a culture of respect and dignity. Leaders must be visible advocates for these values, ensuring that they are woven into the fabric of the school's policies, practices, and daily interactions. This includes providing ongoing training for staff on issues such as cultural competency, anti-bullying techniques, and inclusive teaching strategies.

Leaders also need to be proactive in addressing any instances where respect and dignity may be compromised. This requires a commitment to transparency and accountability, ensuring that all actions taken align with the school's values and policies.

Continuous Reflection and Dialogue

Maintaining an environment of respect and dignity requires continuous reflection and open dialogue. Schools should encourage feedback from students, parents, and teachers on how well they are upholding these values and what improvements could be made. Regularly reviewing and discussing this feedback helps schools to adapt and evolve their practices to better meet the needs of their community.

Fostering respect and dignity in educational settings is fundamental to creating a nurturing and effective learning environment. By implementing practices that promote mutual respect, inclusivity, safety, empathy, and continuous reflection, educators can ensure that all students are treated with the respect and dignity they deserve. This not only supports their academic growth but also their development as compassionate and responsible individuals.

ϷϷϷ

"An educator's role is not to shape minds in their image but to ignite the sparks of curiosity, morality, and independent thought."

❧❧❧

SIX

THE ROLE OF EMPATHY IN TEACHING

Empathy in teaching is a fundamental trait that enhances the educational experience by fostering a deeper connection between educators and students. This emotional understanding helps teachers to meet students' diverse needs more effectively, enhancing their academic and personal growth. Empathy in the educational setting not only aids in classroom management and curriculum delivery but also contributes significantly to developing students' social and emotional skills.

Understanding and Implementing Empathy

Empathy involves the ability to understand and share the feelings of another person. In the context of teaching, this means that educators strive to appreciate the individual experiences and emotions of their students. This understanding can profoundly affect how teachers communicate, discipline, and motivate students, as well as how they tailor educational materials to meet varying needs.

To implement empathy effectively, teachers must first actively listen to their students. This involves paying attention not just to the words being said but also to the emotions and non-verbal cues being expressed. Active listening can provide crucial insights into a student's level of understanding, concerns, and emotional state, enabling teachers to adjust their approach accordingly.

Creating an Emotionally Supportive Classroom Environment

An empathetic teacher creates an emotionally supportive classroom environment that encourages students to express their thoughts and feelings without fear of judgment. This environment can be fostered through various practices such as establishing ground rules that promote respectful communication, regularly checking in with students' emotional well-being, and providing a safe space for sharing personal experiences and concerns.

Such an environment not only supports emotional expression but also builds trust among students and between students and the teacher. Trust is crucial for effective learning, as it makes students more open to engaging with the curriculum and more willing to take intellectual risks.

Empathy and Student Engagement

Empathy directly influences student engagement. When students feel understood and supported, they are more likely to participate actively in class discussions, projects, and other learning activities. Teachers can enhance engagement by demonstrating empathy through personalized feedback on assignments, recognizing individual student struggles and achievements, and adapting lessons to address the unique interests and learning styles of the class.

Furthermore, when empathy is modeled by the teacher, it encourages students to be empathetic towards each other, which can enhance peer-to-peer interactions and collaboration. This can lead to a more inclusive classroom culture, where students feel valued and part of a community.

Empathy in Curriculum Design

Empathy plays a critical role in curriculum design. Educators can use their understanding of students' backgrounds, interests, and emotional states to develop curricula that are relevant and engaging. This might involve integrating topics that reflect the diverse cultures and experiences of the students, or it could include projects that connect with real-world issues relevant to the students' lives.

Incorporating empathy into curriculum design also means being flexible with teaching strategies and materials to accommodate students with different needs, whether these are emotional, physical, or cognitive. This approach ensures that all students have equitable access to learning opportunities.

Challenges and Strategies for Teaching Empathy

Teaching with empathy can present challenges, particularly in diverse classrooms where students come from various backgrounds and have different emotional needs. Teachers must be adept at managing these differences and ensuring that their empathetic actions benefit all students.

To overcome these challenges, educators can engage in professional development focused on emotional intelligence and cultural competence. Workshops, seminars, and collaborative learning with peers can provide teachers with the tools and skills needed to enhance their empathetic understanding.

Additionally, teachers can benefit from reflective practices. By regularly reflecting on their teaching methods and interactions with students, teachers can continuously improve their ability to empathize and adjust their approaches based on what works best for their students.

Empathy and Professional Relationships

The role of empathy extends beyond interactions with students and can significantly affect professional relationships with colleagues and parents. An empathetic teacher is likely to collaborate more effectively with colleagues, leading to a more cohesive work environment and better coordinated efforts to support students. Similarly, empathetic communication with parents can build a partnership that facilitates the educational process and supports students' learning and development at home.

Empathy is a vital component of effective teaching. It enhances the learning environment, boosts student engagement, and is integral to curriculum development. By fostering empathetic relationships and environments, educators not only improve educational outcomes but also contribute to the development of students' social and emotional competencies, preparing them for successful interactions in a complex, diverse world.

ᑭᑭᑭ

"Academic honesty is the cornerstone of a learning environment where trust flourishes and true educational growth is possible."

❧❧❧

SEVEN

SUSTAINABLE TEACHING: ETHICS FOR ENVIRONMENTAL AWARENESS

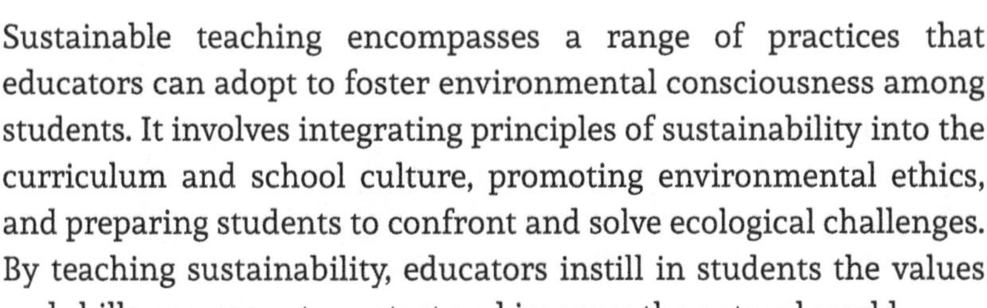

Sustainable teaching encompasses a range of practices that educators can adopt to foster environmental consciousness among students. It involves integrating principles of sustainability into the curriculum and school culture, promoting environmental ethics, and preparing students to confront and solve ecological challenges. By teaching sustainability, educators instill in students the values and skills necessary to protect and improve the natural world.

Foundations of Environmental Ethics in Education

Environmental ethics is a critical component of sustainable teaching. It focuses on the moral relationship between humans and the environment, encouraging respect and care for natural resources. Educators can introduce environmental ethics through discussions about the impact of human activities on the earth and the importance of biodiversity. This foundation helps students understand the ethical implications of environmental degradation and the moral imperatives for conservation and sustainability.

To effectively teach these concepts, educators need to be well-versed in environmental issues and ethics. Professional development in environmental education can equip teachers with the necessary knowledge and resources to incorporate these topics into their teaching effectively.

Integrating Sustainability into the Curriculum

One of the most direct ways to promote sustainability is through curriculum integration. This can be achieved across various subjects, not just science. For example, in social studies, students might explore the relationship between human societies and the environment throughout history or examine different cultural attitudes towards conservation. In literature classes, students can analyze texts that focus on nature or environmental themes.

Mathematics can involve statistical analysis of pollution levels or calculations of carbon footprints, while art classes can use recycled materials or focus on themes of nature and environmental preservation. By weaving environmental topics across different subjects, teachers can reinforce the idea that sustainability is a comprehensive and interdisciplinary challenge.

Project-Based Learning and Environmental Stewardship

Project-based learning (PBL) is an effective pedagogical approach to teach sustainability. PBL involves students in hands-on projects that require them to apply what they have learned to real-world environmental problems. For instance, students might design a school garden that uses permaculture principles, conduct a local water quality study, or develop a recycling program at their school.

These projects not only help students understand environmental concepts in a tangible way but also empower them to become agents of change in their communities. Moreover, by tackling local environmental issues, students can see the immediate impact of their efforts, which can be incredibly motivating and rewarding.

Creating a Sustainable Classroom Environment

Beyond curriculum and projects, sustainable teaching also involves creating a classroom environment that reflects environmental values. This includes using resources wisely, reducing waste, and minimizing energy consumption. Educators can lead by example by implementing recycling systems, using digital documents to reduce paper use, and ensuring that classroom materials are sustainable where possible.

Furthermore, teachers can encourage sustainability by organizing field trips to nature reserves, recycling facilities, or other relevant sites. These experiences provide students with practical insights into environmental management and conservation efforts, enriching their understanding and appreciation of sustainability issues.

Engaging the Wider Community

The effectiveness of sustainable teaching can be enhanced by involving the wider community. Partnerships with local environmental organizations, government agencies, and businesses can provide students with additional resources and learning opportunities. These partnerships might involve guest speakers, community clean-up days, or collaborative projects like tree planting or habitat restoration.

Engaging parents and families in sustainability efforts is also valuable. Schools can host workshops or send home materials that help families adopt more sustainable practices at home. This not only extends the learning environment beyond the classroom but also builds a community-wide commitment to environmental stewardship.

Evaluating and Reflecting on Sustainability Practices

To maintain and improve sustainable teaching practices, continuous evaluation and reflection are necessary. Educators should regularly assess the effectiveness of their sustainability initiatives, seeking feedback from students, colleagues, and the community. Reflection can also involve staying informed about new environmental research and teaching methods, which can enhance the relevance and impact of sustainability education.

Sustainable teaching is an essential element of contemporary education. By embedding environmental ethics into the curriculum, engaging students in meaningful projects, modeling sustainable practices, and involving the community, educators can play a pivotal role in developing the next generation of environmentally conscious citizens. These efforts not only enrich students' academic and ethical development but also contribute to the broader goal of sustainable development.

"Inclusive education recognizes that every student's voice is valuable and that learning is richest when diverse perspectives are embraced."

❦❦❦

EIGHT

THE IMPACT OF TEACHER BIAS ON LEARNING OUTCOMES

Teacher bias, whether conscious or unconscious, can significantly affect learning outcomes by shaping the interactions and expectations between teachers and their students. Bias in educational settings refers to preconceived notions or attitudes towards students based on their race, ethnicity, gender, socio-economic status, or other personal characteristics. Understanding and addressing these biases is crucial for fostering an equitable learning environment where all students can succeed.

Recognizing and Understanding Teacher Bias

The first step in addressing teacher bias is recognizing that it exists. Bias can manifest in various forms, such as lower expectations for students from certain backgrounds, unequal discipline practices, or differential treatment in the allocation of learning opportunities and support. Such biases not only undermine the affected students' educational experiences but can also impact their academic self-esteem and future aspirations.

Educators must engage in self-reflection and be open to training and discussions that help identify and understand their own biases. Professional development workshops, peer discussions, and training in cultural competence are essential tools for educators to explore how their backgrounds and experiences might influence their perceptions and behaviors towards students.

Effects of Bias on Student Performance

Bias can significantly impact student performance and engagement. When students perceive or experience bias, it can lead to decreased motivation, increased anxiety, and lower academic self-efficacy. This is particularly damaging in classrooms where the bias leads to lower expectations for certain students, as these expectations can become self-fulfilling prophecies. Research has shown that students perform better when they feel their teachers have high expectations for them and worse when they perceive the opposite.

Moreover, biased behavior or attitudes can affect the quality of interactions between teachers and students, leading to a breakdown in trust and communication. This undermines the teacher-student relationship, which is a critical factor in effective teaching and learning.

Bias in Assessment and Grading

One of the most direct ways teacher bias can affect learning outcomes is through assessments and grading. Bias may lead teachers to grade students differently based on their perceptions of the student's background rather than the student's actual performance. This can be counteracted by using transparent grading rubrics and involving multiple educators in the assessment process to ensure fairness and objectivity.

Additionally, bias can influence the type and difficulty of tasks assigned to students. Educators might unconsciously offer more challenging and enriching tasks to students they perceive as more capable, often based on their biases, which deprives other students of critical learning opportunities and the chance to demonstrate their abilities.

Strategies to Mitigate the Effects of Bias

To mitigate the effects of teacher bias, educators and institutions can implement several strategies:

Awareness and Education: Regular training on recognizing and combating unconscious bias should be mandatory for all educators. This training should include practical strategies for maintaining objectivity and fairness in classroom interactions, assessments, and discipline.

Diverse Teaching Materials: Using a curriculum that includes diverse perspectives and materials can help challenge stereotypes and reduce bias. Educators should strive to present content that reflects a variety of cultures, backgrounds, and experiences to enrich students' learning and broaden their worldviews.

Structured Reflection: Encouraging teachers to engage in reflective practices can help them examine their teaching methods, decisions, and interactions for potential biases. Keeping reflective journals, participating in peer review sessions, and seeking feedback from students are useful practices.

Peer Observation and Collaboration: Implementing a system where teachers can observe each other's classes and provide feedback can help identify and address bias in classroom practices. Collaboration among teachers can also promote a more unified approach to equitable teaching.

Student Feedback: Regularly collecting feedback from students about their classroom experiences can provide valuable insights into how teaching practices and interactions are perceived, offering an opportunity to adjust practices that may inadvertently perpetuate bias.

Equity Audits: Schools can conduct regular equity audits to examine how well they are providing equal opportunities to all students. These audits can cover various aspects of school operations, including discipline, academic achievement, participation in extracurricular activities, and more.

Teacher bias is a significant barrier to equitable education and can adversely affect learning outcomes. By recognizing and addressing biases, educators can create a classroom environment that fosters fairness, respect, and optimal learning opportunities for all students. Through continued education, reflective practice, and institutional support, biases can be mitigated, leading to a more just and effective educational system.

PPP

"Critical thinking should not be taught merely as a
skill but as a moral imperative, essential for
navigating the complexities of modern life."

ᚦᚦᚦ

NINE

Promoting Critical Thinking through Ethical Dilemmas

Critical thinking is a crucial skill for students in today's complex and rapidly changing world. Teaching students to think critically helps them to not only excel academically but also to become more discerning and reflective individuals. One effective method to foster critical thinking is through the exploration of ethical dilemmas. These dilemmas challenge students to consider multiple perspectives and make reasoned decisions based on ethical reasoning, rather than simple factual recall or personal preference.

Understanding Ethical Dilemmas

Ethical dilemmas are situations in which there is a choice to be made between two options, neither of which resolves the situation in a morally satisfactory manner. These dilemmas often involve a conflict between moral imperatives, where to obey one would result in transgressing another. Introducing students to ethical dilemmas in the classroom setting encourages them to weigh different values and consequences, fostering a deeper understanding of the complexity of moral decision-making.

Integrating Ethical Dilemmas into Curriculum

Ethical dilemmas can be integrated into virtually any subject area. For instance, in literature classes, students might analyze characters' decisions and the moral quandaries they face, while in history, they could examine real-world decisions made by historical figures and the ethical implications of those decisions. In science, discussions could center around the ethics of genetic engineering, artificial intelligence, or environmental conservation. Even mathematics can involve ethical considerations, such as statistics used in public policy decisions or resource allocation.

Teachers can create lessons that specifically focus on ethical dilemmas by presenting hypothetical scenarios or case studies that require students to apply their knowledge and ethical reasoning skills. This approach not only deepens subject matter understanding but also enhances students' ability to apply what they have learned in real-world contexts.

Methods to Teach Ethical Reasoning

To effectively promote critical thinking through ethical dilemmas, educators should employ specific pedagogical strategies. Here are some methods that can be particularly effective:

Socratic Seminar: This method involves creating a dialogue among students where they question and answer each other based on a text or a particular dilemma. The teacher acts as a facilitator, guiding the discussion but allowing students to lead the conversation. This encourages deeper analysis and consideration of differing viewpoints.

Role-Playing: Students assume the roles of different stakeholders in a scenario involving an ethical dilemma. This technique helps students understand the perspectives of others and think about the implications of decisions from multiple viewpoints.

Debate: Organizing formal debates on ethical issues provides students with an opportunity to research and articulate positions on complex topics, defending their views against counterarguments. This not only sharpens their reasoning skills but also their ability to think on their feet.

Reflective Writing: Encouraging students to write about ethical dilemmas and their potential solutions helps them to clarify their thoughts and reflect on the values that influence their decisions. This can be an effective way to solidify the critical thinking process.

Challenges and Solutions in Ethical Discussions

While discussing ethical dilemmas can greatly enhance critical thinking, it also presents certain challenges. These discussions can sometimes lead to conflict or discomfort among students, especially when sensitive or controversial topics are addressed. To manage these challenges, educators should establish clear guidelines for discussion, ensuring that all students feel respected and that their opinions are valued. This includes promoting a classroom culture of respect and openness, where different opinions can be expressed without fear of judgement.

Furthermore, teachers need to be prepared to deal with their own biases and remain neutral, facilitating discussions in a way that all voices are heard and considered. It's also important for educators to be well-versed in conflict resolution techniques to manage any disputes that arise during discussions.

Promoting critical thinking through ethical dilemmas is a powerful pedagogical approach that prepares students for the complexities of modern life. By engaging students with challenging moral questions, educators can help develop not only their cognitive abilities but also their ethical sensibilities. As students learn to navigate these dilemmas, they build essential skills in reasoning, empathy, and decision-making, which are invaluable throughout their educational journey and beyond.

ᐁᐁᐁ

"Reflection is the educator's most powerful tool, turning experience into insight and mistakes into proactive steps toward excellence."

▷▷▷

TEN

THE ETHICS OF ASSESSMENT: FAIRNESS AND OBJECTIVITY

Assessment is a crucial element of education, providing essential feedback on student learning, shaping educational decisions, and influencing future teaching practices. However, the ethical implications of how assessments are designed, implemented, and utilized are significant and complex. Ensuring fairness and objectivity in assessments is not only a matter of technical precision but also of moral importance, as these qualities directly impact educational equity and student success.

Principles of Ethical Assessment

Fairness and objectivity are the pillars of ethical assessment. Fairness involves providing every student an equal opportunity to demonstrate their knowledge and skills, while objectivity requires that assessments are free from bias, allowing for an accurate measure of each student's performance based on agreed-upon standards.

To uphold these principles, educators must ensure that assessments are accessible to all students, including those with disabilities or those who speak languages other than the language of instruction. This might involve providing accommodations such as extra time, alternative formats, or the use of assistive technologies. Fair assessments also mean that the content should be culturally relevant and not disadvantage any group.

Designing Ethical Assessments

The design of assessments is a critical starting point in ensuring their ethical use. Well-designed assessments are aligned with curriculum objectives and accurately reflect the material taught in the classroom. They should also vary in format to cater to different learning styles and abilities, including a mix of multiple-choice questions, essays, projects, and oral presentations.

Moreover, the language used in assessments should be clear and unambiguous to avoid confusion and misinterpretation. The complexity of the language should match the students' age and educational level, ensuring that the assessment measures knowledge of the subject matter, not language proficiency, unless language is the focus of the test.

Avoiding Bias in Assessment

To achieve objectivity, educators must actively work to recognize and eliminate bias in assessments. Bias can occur in many forms—cultural, gender, racial, or socioeconomic—and can skew the accuracy of what the assessments intend to measure. This requires a careful review of test items to ensure they do not favor a particular group of students over others. Engaging a diverse group of educators in the development and review of assessments can help identify and mitigate potential biases.

Another aspect of avoiding bias is the consideration of the halo effect, where a teacher's overall impression of a student might influence the scoring of subjective assessments. To counter this, using anonymous marking where feasible, or having multiple educators grade parts of assessments, can help maintain objectivity.

Ethical Use of Assessment Data

Once assessments are completed, the ethical responsibility extends to how the results are used. Assessment data should be used to support student learning and educational improvement, not to unfairly label, track, or limit students' future learning opportunities.

Data from assessments should be analyzed to identify patterns that might indicate instructional needs, gaps in the curriculum, or areas where teaching methods might be improved. It is also vital that this data is handled with confidentiality and respect for students' privacy and dignity.

Feedback and Communication

An often-overlooked aspect of the ethics of assessment is how results are communicated to students. Feedback should be constructive, aimed at encouraging further learning and development rather than merely pointing out faults. Effective feedback not only details the strengths and weaknesses of the student's performance but also provides specific advice on how to improve.

Communication about assessment results should also involve parents and caregivers, providing them with clear, actionable information about their child's progress and ways they can support their learning at home.

Continuous Reflection and Improvement

Finally, a commitment to the ethics of assessment involves continuous reflection and improvement in assessment practices. Educators should regularly evaluate the effectiveness and fairness of their assessment methods, seeking feedback from students and colleagues and adjusting practices based on current educational research and the diverse needs of their student population.

Ethical assessment practices are crucial for ensuring fairness and objectivity in education. By carefully designing assessments, avoiding biases, using results responsibly, providing constructive feedback, and engaging in continuous improvement, educators can uphold the ethical standards necessary to foster an equitable learning environment. These practices not only contribute to the fairness of educational outcomes but also support the overall integrity of the educational system.

ppp

"The ethical educator sees the classroom as a microcosm of society, where foundational values like fairness and respect are not only taught but embodied."

ϸϸϸ

ELEVEN

TECHNOLOGY AND ETHICS IN MODERN EDUCATION

The integration of technology into modern education has transformed the way teaching and learning occur. While these technological advances offer vast opportunities for enhancing educational experiences, they also bring a host of ethical considerations that educators and institutions must navigate. Issues such as digital equity, privacy, data security, and the ethical use of artificial intelligence and machine learning in educational settings are central to the discourse on technology in education.

Balancing Access and Equity

One of the foremost ethical considerations is the issue of access and equity. As technology becomes increasingly embedded in educational practices, ensuring that all students have equal access to these tools is crucial. This involves more than just providing devices; it also includes access to reliable internet services, digital content that is accessible to students with disabilities, and the provision of training for students and teachers to effectively use these technologies.

Schools and educational institutions need to address the digital divide—the gap between those who have ready access to computers and the internet, and those who do not. This gap often reflects and amplifies existing socioeconomic and regional disparities, potentially exacerbating educational inequalities. Strategies to bridge the digital divide may include lending programs for devices, subsidized internet access for low-income families, and investing in digital infrastructure in underserved areas.

Privacy and Data Security

The use of technology in education also raises significant concerns about privacy and data security. Educational technologies often collect vast amounts of data from students, including personal information, learning progress, and behavioral patterns. The ethical handling of this data is paramount. Educators and technology providers must ensure that data is collected, stored, and used in ways that respect student privacy and comply with legal standards such as the General Data Protection Regulation (GDPR) in the European Union and the Children's Online Privacy Protection Act (COPPA) in the United States.

It is essential for educational institutions to be transparent with students and parents about what data is being collected and how it will be used. Consent should be obtained in a manner that is informed and voluntary, and students and parents should have options to opt-out where appropriate.

Ethical Use of Artificial Intelligence

The deployment of artificial intelligence (AI) and machine learning technologies in education brings about a unique set of ethical issues. AI can be used for personalized learning, where algorithms adjust the difficulty level of tasks based on the student's performance, or for automated grading and feedback systems. While these technologies can enhance learning efficiency and provide insights into student performance, they also raise questions about the accuracy and fairness of algorithmic decision-making.

There is a risk that AI systems may perpetuate existing biases if they are trained on biased data sets. For instance, an AI system that develops learning pathways based on data from students who have traditionally excelled might not effectively serve students who have different learning needs. To combat this, AI systems must be designed and regularly audited for biases and their algorithms should be as transparent as possible.

Digital Citizenship and Ethical Use of Resources

As students spend more time online, teaching digital citizenship—responsible and ethical behavior in a digital world—becomes increasingly important. This includes understanding how to safely and respectfully use technology, recognizing and responding to cyberbullying, understanding copyright and intellectual property rights, and knowing how to evaluate the reliability of online information.

Educators must also consider the environmental impact of technology. The ethical use of technological resources includes efforts to minimize waste related to technology, such as energy consumption and the disposal of electronic waste. Encouraging sustainable practices, such as recycling old devices and using energy-efficient technologies, is also part of ethical responsibility in education.

The ethical integration of technology into education requires careful consideration of access and equity, privacy and data protection, the responsible use of artificial intelligence, and the cultivation of digital citizenship. By addressing these ethical issues thoughtfully and proactively, educators can harness the benefits of technology to enhance educational outcomes while safeguarding the rights and well-being of all students. These efforts ensure that technology serves as a tool for educational advancement rather than a source of inequity or harm.

"Building trust in educational settings starts with transparency, where students not only know what to expect but also feel their voices are heard and valued."

❦❦❦

TWELVE

ADDRESSING CHEATING AND ACADEMIC DISHONESTY

Cheating and academic dishonesty are significant challenges in educational environments, threatening the integrity of educational institutions and undermining the value of learning. Addressing these issues requires a multifaceted approach that combines clear policies, effective prevention strategies, and educational efforts to promote academic integrity.

Understanding the Roots of Academic Dishonesty

To effectively address cheating, it is crucial to understand its root causes. Academic dishonesty often stems from several factors, including pressure to succeed, a lack of preparation, perceived unfairness in assessment, and a culture that may inadvertently encourage or tolerate cheating. Understanding these factors can help educators develop more effective strategies to prevent dishonest behavior.

Developing a Culture of Integrity

Creating a culture of integrity within educational institutions is foundational in combating academic dishonesty. This involves more than just having honor codes or strict rules; it requires cultivating an environment where ethical behavior is valued and reinforced through every aspect of educational practice. Educators and administrators need to model integrity in their actions and decisions, making clear that ethical behavior is expected and valued.

Incorporating discussions about ethics and integrity into the curriculum can also help instill these values. Courses and workshops that discuss academic honesty, the consequences of cheating, and the importance of ethical behavior in professional and personal settings can be particularly effective.

Clear Policies and Expectations

Clear, well-communicated policies and expectations are critical to preventing academic dishonesty. Students should understand what constitutes cheating, why it is prohibited, and what the consequences are for engaging in such behavior. These policies should be consistently enforced to maintain their effectiveness and to demonstrate the institution's commitment to integrity.

Policies should also include guidelines for proper citation practices and explanations of plagiarism to ensure students understand how to appropriately use and credit sources. Education about what constitutes plagiarism and how to avoid it is essential, as misunderstandings about these issues can lead to unintentional academic dishonesty.

Preventive Measures

Preventive measures are key to reducing the incidence of cheating. This can include designing assessments that are difficult to cheat on, such as those requiring analysis and critical thinking rather than simple recall of facts. Changing assessment formats regularly and personalizing questions can also help limit opportunities for dishonesty.

Technology can play a role in prevention as well. The use of plagiarism detection software, secure testing environments, and other technological tools can help identify instances of cheating and deter students from attempting to cheat.

Support Systems for Students

Providing adequate support systems for students can help prevent academic dishonesty by addressing some of the pressures that lead to cheating. Access to tutoring services, writing centers, and time management workshops can help students cope with academic challenges in an honest and effective manner. Ensuring that the workload is reasonable and that assessments are fair can also reduce the stress that may lead students to consider cheating.

Addressing Cases of Academic Dishonesty

When instances of academic dishonesty do occur, they should be addressed promptly and fairly. The process for handling such cases should be transparent and consistent, ensuring that all students are treated equitably. Consequences should be clearly linked to the nature and severity of the cheating incident.

Restorative practices may also be employed, focusing on helping students understand the impact of their actions and learn from their mistakes. These practices can involve reflective exercises, meetings with advisors, or participation in ethics seminars, which help rehabilitate students rather than solely punishing them.

Addressing cheating and academic dishonesty in educational settings requires a comprehensive approach that includes understanding the causes of dishonest behavior, creating a culture of integrity, establishing clear policies, implementing preventive measures, providing student support systems, and dealing with incidents effectively and fairly. By tackling academic dishonesty from multiple angles, educational institutions can uphold the standards of integrity that are essential to the value and efficacy of education.

ᐅᐅᐅ

"Professional development in ethics is not just about avoiding pitfalls but about aspiring to elevate one's practice to the pinnacle of professional integrity."

▷▷▷

THIRTEEN

Collaborative Learning: Ethics in Group Work

Collaborative learning is a pedagogical approach that involves students working together to solve problems, complete tasks, or learn new concepts. While collaboration offers numerous educational benefits, including enhanced problem-solving abilities and improved communication skills, it also raises important ethical considerations. Ensuring fairness, accountability, and respectful interactions in group work settings is essential to maintain the integrity and effectiveness of collaborative learning environments.

Promoting Fairness in Group Work

Fairness is a critical aspect of collaborative learning. All members of a group should have equal opportunities to contribute to the project and share the benefits of the group's success. Educators can promote fairness by clearly defining the roles and responsibilities of each group member, ensuring that workloads are evenly distributed, and setting up structures that allow every student to voice their ideas and concerns.

One effective strategy is to rotate roles within the group throughout the course of a project. This approach not only prevents any single student from monopolizing a certain aspect of the work but also helps all members develop a range of skills and perspectives. Additionally, providing clear rubrics that outline the expectations for each role can help students understand what is required of them and how they will be assessed.

Ensuring Accountability in Collaborative Settings

Accountability in group work ensures that all members contribute appropriately and that individual efforts are recognized. Educators can foster accountability by establishing checkpoints throughout the duration of a project where each student's contributions are assessed and discussed. This might involve interim reports, presentations, or reflective essays that require students to describe their roles and contributions.

Using peer evaluation forms can also be an effective way to hold students accountable. These forms allow group members to assess each other's contributions, which can be factored into the final grades. Such evaluations should be guided by criteria established at the outset of the project to ensure they are fair and objective.

Encouraging Ethical Collaboration

Ethical collaboration involves more than just sharing work; it requires a commitment to honesty, integrity, and respect. Educators must instill these values in their students to ensure that collaborative learning experiences are positive and productive. This involves teaching students to respect diverse viewpoints, negotiate differences constructively, and engage in honest communication.

Creating a classroom culture that values ethical behavior can be supported by explicit instruction in teamwork and ethics at the start of any collaborative project. Discussions or workshops that address common ethical issues in group work, such as free-riding, conflict resolution, and equitable participation, can prepare students for the challenges of collaborative assignments.

Dealing with Conflicts in Group Dynamics

Conflict is a natural part of any collaborative effort, but how it is managed can significantly impact the ethical climate of group work. Educators should provide students with strategies for constructive conflict resolution, such as active listening, seeking common ground, and using structured negotiation techniques. Training students in these methods can help prevent conflicts from becoming personal and ensure that they are resolved in a way that is fair to all parties involved.

Moreover, educators should be prepared to intervene in group conflicts when necessary. While it is important for students to develop their own conflict resolution skills, instructor oversight can help ensure that conflicts are resolved ethically and that no student is marginalized or bullied.

Assessing Group Work Ethically

The assessment of group work must also be handled with care to ensure it is fair and reflective of each student's contributions. This might involve a combination of individual and group grades, where part of the students' marks come from the group's overall performance and part from their individual contributions. Such a hybrid approach can help balance the need to assess collaborative outcomes with the need to recognize individual efforts.

Clear communication about how group work will be assessed is vital. Students should understand from the beginning of the project how their grades will be determined and what aspects of their performance will be evaluated. This transparency helps prevent misunderstandings and anxiety about the grading process.

Collaborative learning can be a highly effective educational method, but it requires careful attention to ethical considerations. By promoting fairness, ensuring accountability, encouraging ethical collaboration, managing conflicts constructively, and assessing group work carefully, educators can maximize the benefits of collaborative learning while maintaining a respectful and productive learning environment. These efforts not only enhance the learning experience but also prepare students to work effectively and ethically in their future professional and personal lives.

ppp

"Digital equity is not just about having access to technology but about ensuring that every student can use that technology to unlock their potential."

❧❧❧

FOURTEEN

ETHICAL CHALLENGES IN DISTANCE LEARNING

Distance learning has become an increasingly common mode of education, particularly highlighted by the global shift toward online learning due to public health concerns. While it offers flexibility and accessibility, it also introduces a range of ethical challenges that educators and institutions must navigate carefully. These challenges include ensuring equity, maintaining academic integrity, safeguarding privacy, and providing adequate support to students.

Ensuring Equity in Access to Distance Learning

One of the primary ethical concerns in distance learning is equity in access. Not all students have the same access to technology, high-speed internet, or a conducive learning environment at home. Educational institutions have a responsibility to address these disparities to ensure that all students have an equal opportunity to participate in and benefit from distance learning.

To mitigate these inequities, schools can provide devices like tablets or laptops to students who need them and negotiate with internet service providers for discounted or donated services. Additionally, providing alternatives such as downloadable resources that do not require continuous internet access can help bridge the gap for students with limited connectivity.

Maintaining Academic Integrity

Academic integrity is another significant challenge in the context of distance learning. The remote nature of learning can make it more difficult to monitor exams and assessments, increasing opportunities for academic dishonesty. To address this, educators can employ various strategies such as modifying assessment methods to focus more on essays, open-book exams, and projects that require demonstration of applied knowledge, which are less prone to cheating than traditional exams.

Additionally, institutions can utilize technology such as plagiarism detection software and proctoring tools that monitor exams through webcams. However, the use of such technologies introduces another layer of ethical consideration regarding student privacy.

Privacy and Data Security

The protection of student data is a critical issue in distance learning, where much of the communication and submission of work occur over digital platforms. Educators and institutions must ensure that the technologies used comply with data protection laws and regulations, such as the General Data Protection Regulation (GDPR) in the European Union or the Family Educational Rights and Privacy Act (FERPA) in the United States.

Privacy concerns are not limited to the security of data but also involve the privacy of students' personal spaces, which become visible in video conferencing. Educators must be sensitive to the exposure this brings and encourage, but not require, the use of video, providing guidelines on how to maintain professionalism and privacy.

Providing Adequate Student Support

Distance learning can often lead to students feeling isolated, which can affect their mental health and academic performance. Providing adequate support is therefore an ethical imperative. This support can take various forms, including regular virtual office hours, online tutoring services, and accessible communication channels that allow students to reach out for help when needed.

Institutions should also provide resources for mental health support, such as online counseling or workshops on managing stress and anxiety. Educators can contribute by creating an engaging and supportive online community, where students are encouraged to interact with each other and participate in online forums or group discussions.

Adapting Teaching Methods for Effective Distance Learning

The effectiveness of distance learning depends significantly on the adaptation of teaching methods to suit the online format. This involves not only using the right tools but also adjusting pedagogical approaches to engage students and enhance their learning experience. Educators need to be trained in effective online teaching strategies and familiar with the digital tools that facilitate interactive and inclusive learning.

Assessment and Feedback in Distance Learning

Assessing student progress and providing feedback in a distance learning environment require careful consideration to ensure they are fair and timely. Since traditional methods of assessment may not always be appropriate, alternative forms of assessment that allow for demonstration of comprehension and skills are necessary. These could include portfolios, presentations, and peer-reviewed assignments.

Feedback, which is crucial for student learning, should be constructive and frequent to help students stay engaged and motivated. Digital tools that track progress and automate feedback can be useful, but they should be used judiciously to ensure that personalized feedback is not lost.

Ethical challenges in distance learning are multifaceted and require a proactive approach from educational institutions and educators. By ensuring equitable access, maintaining academic integrity, protecting privacy, providing adequate support, adapting teaching methods, and effectively assessing and providing feedback, educators can uphold ethical standards and enhance the quality and fairness of distance learning. These efforts are essential in fostering an educational environment that is both effective and respectful of students' rights and needs.

ᗭᗭᗭ

"Teaching is an act of hope—a belief that the lessons imparted today will germinate into tomorrow's solutions, innovations, and progress."

ᐁᐁᐁ

FIFTEEN

DEVELOPING ETHICAL LEADERS THROUGH EDUCATION

The role of education in shaping future leaders is immense, with a particular responsibility to cultivate ethical leadership. Ethical leaders are crucial for all sectors of society, as they influence positive changes, foster trust, and demonstrate integrity. The educational system, from primary schools to higher education institutions, plays a key role in developing the character and skills necessary for ethical leadership.

Foundations of Ethical Leadership

Ethical leadership starts with a foundation of core values such as integrity, honesty, fairness, respect, and social responsibility. Educational institutions are ideally positioned to instill these values early and reinforce them continuously throughout a student's academic journey. This can be achieved through both curriculum design and the cultivation of a school culture that prioritizes ethical behavior and decision-making.

Curriculum that incorporates ethics and leadership can be integrated into a wide range of subjects. For instance, literature classes can analyze characters and plot decisions through the lens of moral complexity, while history lessons can include studies of leaders who have made significant ethical or unethical decisions and the consequences of those decisions.

Role Models and Mentoring

Teachers and administrators often serve as role models for ethical behavior. Their daily interactions with students can reinforce the importance of ethics in leadership. Educators must be conscious of this role and strive to demonstrate ethical behavior in all their professional duties. This includes being transparent about decision-making processes, treating all students equitably, and handling conflicts and challenges with integrity.

Mentoring programs can also play a vital role in developing ethical leaders. By pairing students with mentors who exemplify ethical leadership, educational institutions provide models of how these values are enacted in real-world scenarios. Mentors can guide students in understanding complex ethical dilemmas, making difficult decisions, and reflecting on the consequences of their actions.

Critical Thinking and Ethical Decision-Making

Critical thinking is integral to ethical leadership. Educators can foster this by challenging students to think deeply about ethical issues, encouraging them to ask questions and explore different perspectives. This could be facilitated through case studies, simulations, and role-playing exercises that require students to navigate complex ethical landscapes and make decisions based on their understanding of ethical principles.

These activities help students develop a nuanced understanding of ethics and leadership, including recognizing the often-competing interests and values that leaders must balance. It also prepares them to deal with ambiguity and uncertainty in decision-making, skills that are essential for ethical leaders.

Service Learning and Community Engagement

Service learning integrates meaningful community service with instruction and reflection to enrich the learning experience, teach civic responsibility, and strengthen communities. Through service learning, students apply academic skills to solve real-world problems, all while considering the ethical dimensions of their actions.

Such programs not only provide practical experience in leadership but also emphasize the impact of ethical leadership on communities. Students learn the importance of considering the broader consequences of their decisions and the ways in which leaders can contribute positively to society.

Encouraging a Culture of Feedback and Reflection

Developing ethical leaders requires an environment where feedback and reflection are valued. Educational settings should encourage students to seek and thoughtfully consider feedback on their ethical decision-making and leadership styles. This could be supported through peer feedback systems, reflective journals, and opportunities for revising decisions and approaches based on feedback.

Reflection is a critical component of ethical leadership development. By regularly reflecting on their experiences and the outcomes of their decisions, students can deepen their understanding of how their actions align with ethical principles and where they might need to make adjustments.

Assessment and Evaluation of Ethical Leadership

Assessing students' development as ethical leaders can be challenging, but it is essential for providing targeted educational interventions. Educators can employ a variety of assessment methods, such as portfolio assessments, which include a collection of a student's work that provides insight into their growth in ethical reasoning and leadership capabilities.

Developing ethical leaders through education is a multifaceted endeavor that requires a commitment from educational institutions to integrate ethics throughout their teaching and culture. By embedding ethical considerations into the curriculum, providing role models and mentors, promoting critical thinking and decision-making, facilitating service learning, and fostering a culture of feedback and reflection, schools can cultivate leaders who are prepared to act with integrity and responsibility. These efforts are crucial in shaping the future of society, ensuring that the next generation of leaders is equipped to handle the ethical challenges they will face.

ᗰᗰᗰ

"Ethical dilemmas in the classroom are not obstacles but opportunities to teach some of life's most valuable lessons about judgment and character."

ᐅᐅᐅ

SIXTEEN

Privacy Rights of Students and Educators

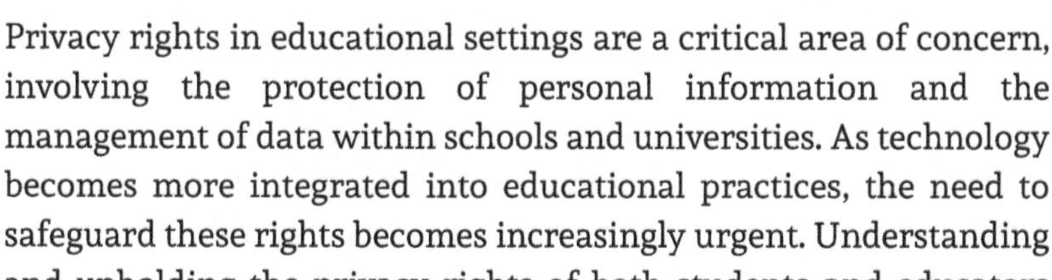

Privacy rights in educational settings are a critical area of concern, involving the protection of personal information and the management of data within schools and universities. As technology becomes more integrated into educational practices, the need to safeguard these rights becomes increasingly urgent. Understanding and upholding the privacy rights of both students and educators are essential for maintaining trust, respect, and integrity within educational institutions.

Understanding Privacy Rights in Education

Privacy rights in education primarily concern the protection of personal information. This includes data such as grades, medical information, personal identification details, and other sensitive information that could have significant implications if mishandled. For students, the protection of privacy also extends to their personal lives, which can be exposed to scrutiny in digital environments, such as online classrooms or social media.

For educators, privacy rights include the protection of their personal information and professional data, such as employment records, performance evaluations, and other sensitive material. Additionally, educators must navigate the privacy of their interactions with students and colleagues, which can be complicated by the use of digital communication tools.

Legal Frameworks Governing Privacy

Several legal frameworks govern privacy rights in educational settings. In the United States, the Family Educational Rights and Privacy Act (FERPA) provides students with rights to access their educational records and limits the disclosure of these records without consent. Similarly, the General Data Protection Regulation (GDPR) in the European Union sets strict guidelines for data protection and grants individuals rights over their personal data, including the right to access, correct, and delete their data.

Educational institutions must ensure compliance with these and other relevant laws, adapting their policies and practices to safeguard privacy rights effectively. This involves training staff on legal requirements and best practices for data protection and establishing clear protocols for handling personal information.

Challenges Posed by Technology

The integration of technology in education brings numerous benefits but also poses significant privacy challenges. Online learning platforms, digital communication tools, and student information systems collect and store vast amounts of data. The risk of data breaches or inappropriate use of data is a constant concern.

To address these challenges, institutions must implement robust cybersecurity measures, including secure data storage solutions, encryption, and regular security audits. Educators should be particularly cautious with the use of technologies that monitor student activity, such as surveillance software or online proctoring tools, ensuring that they do not infringe on students' privacy rights unnecessarily.

Privacy in Digital Communications

Digital communications between students and educators, such as emails, chat messages, and video calls, must be conducted with a high degree of privacy and professionalism. Institutions should provide secure platforms for communication and set clear guidelines on the appropriate use of digital tools.

Educators should be trained on the implications of digital communications for privacy, including understanding how to manage digital records and maintain confidentiality when discussing sensitive issues electronically.

Educational Data and Third-Party Services

Many educational institutions rely on third-party services for functions such as data management, online learning, and student assessments. Contracts with these providers must include strict privacy protections and compliance with relevant privacy laws. Institutions need to conduct thorough due diligence on third-party providers to ensure they meet these standards.

Rights to Privacy Education

Part of protecting privacy rights involves educating students and educators about their rights and responsibilities related to privacy. This includes training on the safe use of technology, understanding the rights to access and control over personal data, and recognizing potential privacy risks.

Developing a Culture of Privacy

Ultimately, protecting privacy rights in education requires developing a culture of privacy that emphasizes respect for personal information and conscientious data management. This culture should be supported by clear policies, regular training, and a commitment to transparency and accountability in all data-related practices.

The privacy rights of students and educators are foundational to the ethical functioning of educational institutions. By understanding and addressing the complexities of privacy in the digital age, respecting legal frameworks, and fostering a culture of privacy, educational institutions can protect these essential rights. Such efforts ensure that the educational environment remains a safe and respectful space for both learning and personal development.

ϸϸϸ

"Every student has a unique journey; an educator's job is to pave a path that respects their individuality while challenging them to grow."

❧❧❧

SEVENTEEN

BALANCING AUTHORITY AND AUTONOMY IN EDUCATION

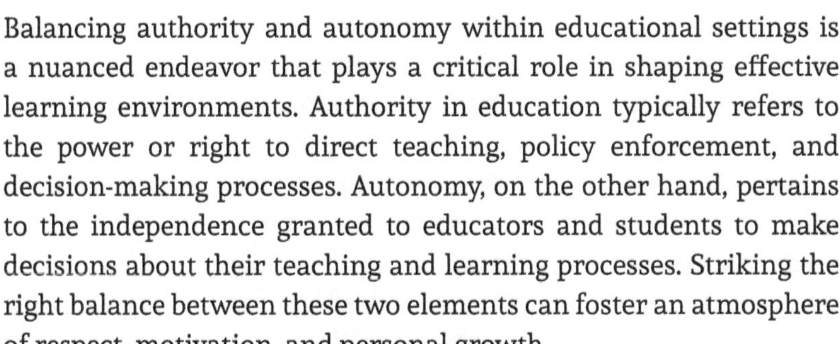

Balancing authority and autonomy within educational settings is a nuanced endeavor that plays a critical role in shaping effective learning environments. Authority in education typically refers to the power or right to direct teaching, policy enforcement, and decision-making processes. Autonomy, on the other hand, pertains to the independence granted to educators and students to make decisions about their teaching and learning processes. Striking the right balance between these two elements can foster an atmosphere of respect, motivation, and personal growth.

The Importance of Authority in Educational Settings

Authority is essential in educational environments as it establishes a framework within which learning can occur. Teachers, administrators, and educational policies provide the structure needed to guide student learning, maintain discipline, and uphold standards that ensure the educational institution functions smoothly and efficiently. Authority also plays a role in curriculum development, the establishment of grading systems, and the enforcement of rules that protect the welfare and safety of all members of the school community.

However, excessive authority can lead to a rigid and stifling environment where creativity and personal expression are curtailed. When students feel overly controlled, their motivation to engage with the learning process can diminish, and they may not develop critical life skills such as decision-making and problem-solving.

Encouraging Autonomy in Learning

Autonomy in education refers to the degree of control that teachers and students have over the learning experience. Autonomy for educators involves the ability to choose teaching methods, curricular materials, and assessment techniques that they believe will best meet their students' needs. For students, autonomy might include choices about what projects to undertake, how to approach learning tasks, or even aspects of classroom management.

Research has shown that when students are given more autonomy, they are more engaged, motivated, and likely to enjoy learning. Autonomy supports the development of self-regulation skills and can lead to deeper, more personalized learning experiences. It encourages students to take responsibility for their education and to become active participants rather than passive recipients.

Strategies for Balancing Authority and Autonomy

To achieve an effective balance between authority and autonomy, educational leaders and teachers can employ several strategies:

Democratic Teaching Practices: Incorporating democratic teaching practices involves students in decision-making processes related to their learning. This might include setting classroom rules together, choosing topics for study, or selecting methods for projects. Such practices help balance teacher authority with student autonomy, fostering a collaborative learning environment.

Flexible Policy Implementation: While policies are necessary for the smooth operation of educational institutions, allowing some flexibility in their implementation can help accommodate individual needs. Teachers should have the discretion to adapt policies in ways that support effective teaching and respond to students' varying academic and emotional needs.

Professional Autonomy for Teachers: Supporting professional autonomy for teachers can lead to more innovative and responsive teaching practices. Teachers who feel empowered to make instructional decisions are more likely to be committed to and enthusiastic about their work, benefiting their students. Professional development opportunities that enhance teachers' skills in classroom management, curriculum design, and pedagogy can further support this autonomy.

Encouraging Student-Led Learning: Techniques such as project-based learning, inquiry-based learning, and flipped classrooms can increase student autonomy. These methods allow students to explore subjects of interest deeply, control the pace of their learning, and engage in active problem-solving.

Mentoring and Guidance: While promoting autonomy, it's crucial to provide mentoring and guidance to ensure that students and teachers are supported in their decisions. This can involve regular feedback, access to resources, and opportunities for reflection and discussion about their choices and actions.

Balancing Responsibilities with Rights: Educators should teach students that with autonomy comes responsibility. Understanding that their choices have consequences can help students make more thoughtful and informed decisions.

Balancing authority and autonomy in education is essential for creating a learning environment that fosters independence, encourages engagement, and respects the guiding structures of educational institutions. By implementing strategies that promote both teacher and student autonomy within a framework of clear, flexible authority, educators can optimize learning outcomes and prepare students for the responsibilities of academic and life challenges outside the classroom. This balance not only enhances educational effectiveness but also supports the overall development of students as autonomous and ethical individuals.

"A curriculum that embraces cultural diversity teaches students not only to see the world but also to engage with it empathetically and ethically."

▷▷▷

EIGHTEEN

ETHICAL CONSIDERATIONS IN CURRICULUM DEVELOPMENT

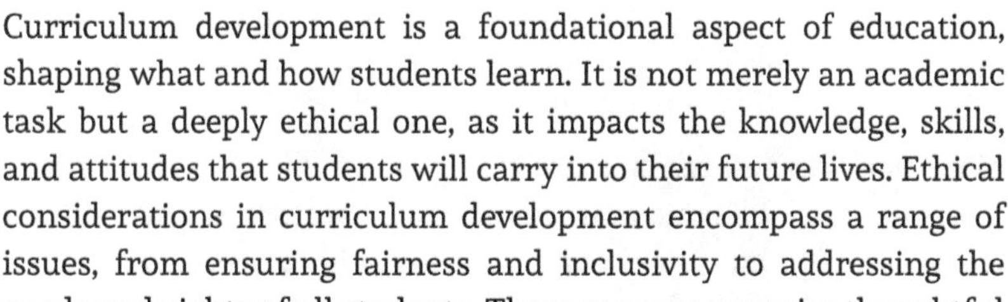

Curriculum development is a foundational aspect of education, shaping what and how students learn. It is not merely an academic task but a deeply ethical one, as it impacts the knowledge, skills, and attitudes that students will carry into their future lives. Ethical considerations in curriculum development encompass a range of issues, from ensuring fairness and inclusivity to addressing the needs and rights of all students. These concerns require thoughtful engagement and deliberate decision-making by educators and curriculum developers.

Ensuring Inclusivity and Representation

One of the primary ethical considerations in curriculum development is inclusivity. An inclusive curriculum reflects a diverse array of cultural, historical, and personal perspectives, providing all students with materials that acknowledge and respect their identities and experiences. This means incorporating texts, examples, and case studies that represent a variety of races, ethnicities, genders, religions, and other societal and personal characteristics.

Inclusivity also involves addressing different learning needs. Curriculum developers must consider students with disabilities by incorporating accessible materials and learning strategies that accommodate diverse learners, ensuring that all students have an equal opportunity to succeed.

Fairness in Content Selection

Fairness in curriculum development involves more than just balanced representation; it also concerns the impartiality of content and the avoidance of bias. Curriculum developers must critically evaluate resources to ensure that they do not perpetuate stereotypes or provide slanted views of history and science. This requires a commitment to presenting information that is fact-based and unbiased, allowing students to form their own informed opinions.

Moreover, fairness entails providing students with a balanced understanding of controversial issues. Educators should aim to teach students how to engage critically with various viewpoints and develop reasoned arguments, preparing them for informed citizenship in a diverse society.

Cultural Sensitivity and Relevance

Curriculum content must be culturally sensitive, acknowledging and valuing the backgrounds of all students. This sensitivity helps in creating an environment where students feel respected and valued, which is crucial for their engagement and learning. Culturally relevant pedagogy not only enhances student motivation but also helps in building connections between students' lives and their learning materials.

Additionally, curriculum developers must be aware of the historical and cultural contexts of the content they include. This is particularly important when dealing with historical events or cultural practices that may be sensitive. Educators need to handle such topics with care, ensuring that they are taught in a way that is both respectful and enlightening.

Ethics of Technology Integration

The integration of technology into the curriculum raises its own set of ethical considerations. While technology can greatly enhance learning experiences, it also introduces issues related to digital equity, privacy, and the potential for distraction and misuse. Curriculum developers must consider these factors when incorporating digital tools and resources, ensuring that all students have equitable access to technology and that their privacy is protected.

Environmental Ethics in Curriculum Development

Another important aspect of ethical curriculum development is the incorporation of environmental education. As global environmental issues continue to escalate, educating students about their role in sustainability and environmental stewardship becomes increasingly crucial. Curriculum developers have the responsibility to integrate topics that teach students about environmental impacts, sustainability practices, and the ethical implications of human interactions with the environment.

Professional Ethics and Continuous Improvement

Curriculum developers must adhere to high professional standards, maintaining integrity in their work and continually seeking to improve the curriculum based on feedback and new research. This involves regular reviews and updates to the curriculum to ensure that it remains relevant, accurate, and effective in meeting the educational needs of students.

The process of curriculum development should also include consultations with a wide range of stakeholders including teachers, students, parents, and community members. These consultations can provide diverse perspectives and help ensure that the curriculum meets the educational and ethical needs of the community.

Ethical considerations in curriculum development are essential for creating educational materials that are fair, inclusive, and respectful of all students. By addressing these ethical issues, educators can develop curricula that not only convey important knowledge and skills but also foster social and moral responsibility. This approach to curriculum development not only enhances the learning experience for students but also contributes to the development of a more just and informed society.

ppp

*"The role of an educator is akin to a gardener,
nurturing potential not by controlling growth but
by providing a nourishing environment."*

❧❧❧

NINETEEN

BUILDING TRUST IN EDUCATIONAL RELATIONSHIPS

Trust is a foundational element in educational relationships, underpinning effective teaching, learning, and collaboration within schools and universities. Whether it's the trust between students and teachers, among peers, or between educators and parents, building and maintaining trust enhances educational outcomes and creates a positive, supportive environment. Here, we delve into the importance of trust in educational settings, the challenges to building it, and strategies for fostering trustworthy relationships.

The Importance of Trust in Education

Trust influences nearly every aspect of the educational experience. It affects students' willingness to engage in learning, their comfort in taking intellectual risks, and their ability to be open about their challenges. For teachers, trust in their professional relationships can affect their job satisfaction, their willingness to collaborate with colleagues, and their capacity to innovate in their teaching practices.

In the broader school community, trust plays a critical role in the effectiveness of communication between schools and families, the implementation of school policies, and the community's overall support for the school's mission.

Challenges to Building Trust

Several challenges can impede the development of trust in educational settings:

Communication Barriers: Misunderstandings or a lack of communication can lead to mistrust. This can be particularly significant in diverse educational environments where language, cultural differences, and different communication styles can complicate interactions.

Previous Negative Experiences: Students or parents who have had negative experiences with educational institutions may be less likely to trust. This can be due to perceived or actual biases, poor handling of past situations, or inconsistency in educational delivery.

Lack of Consistency: Inconsistency in enforcing rules, delivering curriculum, or interacting with students and parents can undermine trust. Consistency in behavior and policy implementation tells students and parents what to expect and helps to build a stable, trustworthy environment.

Perceived Incompetence or Unfairness: If students or parents perceive that teachers or administrators are not competent or are unfair in their dealings, trust can quickly erode.

Strategies for Building Trust

Building trust in educational settings involves intentional strategies and practices:

Clear, Open Communication: Effective communication is the cornerstone of trust. This means being transparent about policies, decisions, and educational practices. Regular updates, open lines of communication, and forums for feedback all contribute to an atmosphere of openness.

Consistency in Actions and Policies: Consistency in enforcing rules, grading, and classroom management practices helps create a predictable environment. When students and parents know what to expect, they are more likely to trust the educational system and its administrators.

Professional Competence: Teachers and administrators need to demonstrate competence in their roles. This includes not only mastery of subject matter but also effective teaching strategies, fair assessment practices, and adept handling of administrative duties.

Respectful Interactions: Showing respect in every interaction within the educational environment, regardless of differences in opinion, background, or personal characteristics, is essential for building trust. This includes listening actively, valuing input from students and parents, and addressing concerns promptly and fairly.

Empathy and Support: Demonstrating empathy involves understanding and being sensitive to the personal and academic struggles that students and parents might face. Supportive actions, such as providing academic help or counseling resources, strengthen trust by showing commitment to the welfare of students and families.

Involvement and Engagement: Encouraging parent and community involvement in school activities can build trust. When parents and community members are actively engaged in the educational process, they gain a better understanding of the challenges and successes of the school, fostering a greater trust.

Building Personal Relationships: Taking time to get to know students and parents personally can transform educational relationships. This might include conversations about non-academic interests, attending community events, or simple gestures of recognition and appreciation.

Professional Development: Ongoing professional development can help educators improve their skills in building trust. Workshops on communication, diversity, classroom management, and conflict resolution can equip teachers with the tools they need to create trustworthy relationships.

Trust is essential for creating a thriving educational environment. By focusing on clear communication, consistent practices, professional competence, respectful interactions, empathy, engagement, personal relationships, and continuous professional development, educators can build and maintain trust. These efforts not only enhance the educational experience but also lay the groundwork for students to develop into trustworthy individuals in their own right, equipped to build positive relationships in all areas of their lives.

ᕀᕀᕀ

"Feedback in education should be a mirror,
reflecting both the strengths and areas for growth,
always with the aim of guiding and supporting."

ϸϸϸ

TWENTY

REFLECTION AND GROWTH: THE ETHICAL DEVELOPMENT OF EDUCATORS

The ethical development of educators is an ongoing process that requires continuous reflection and growth. This development is crucial not only for personal and professional integrity but also for fostering an educational environment that promotes equity, respect, and quality learning. By engaging in regular reflection and actively pursuing growth opportunities, educators can enhance their understanding and practice of ethical teaching, which in turn profoundly impacts their students' educational experiences.

Understanding the Importance of Ethical Reflection

Ethical reflection involves examining one's own teaching practices, decisions, and interactions from an ethical standpoint. This reflective process helps educators recognize the complex moral dimensions of teaching and understand how their values influence their professional actions. Reflecting on ethics allows educators to critically assess their behavior and choices, ensuring they align with the ethical standards of the profession and the needs of their students.

Developing a Framework for Ethical Reflection

To systematically engage in ethical reflection, educators can develop a personal framework that guides their reflective practices. This might involve setting aside regular times for reflection, keeping a journal, or engaging in discussions with peers. The framework should include consideration of several key aspects:

Equity: Reflecting on how to ensure equitable treatment and opportunities for all students.

Respect: Considering the ways respect is shown to students, colleagues, and oneself.

Integrity: Assessing the consistency between one's values and actions.

Professionalism: Evaluating adherence to professional standards and ongoing professional development.

The Role of Moral Philosophy in Education

Educators' ethical development can be enriched by studying moral philosophy, which provides a broader understanding of ethical theories and principles. Engaging with philosophical ideas about morality, justice, and the good life can help educators form a well-rounded ethical viewpoint that informs their teaching philosophy and practices.

Case Studies and Ethical Dilemmas

One effective method for deepening ethical understanding is through the analysis of case studies and ethical dilemmas related to education. These studies can be used in professional development settings to help educators practice applying ethical principles to complex, real-world situations. Discussing these scenarios with peers provides multiple perspectives and can lead to more nuanced understanding and better problem-solving strategies.

Feedback and Evaluation

Feedback from students, peers, and supervisors is invaluable for ethical development. Educators can encourage honest feedback by creating open, trusting relationships within their professional community. Regular performance evaluations, when approached from a growth mindset, can also provide critical insights into areas where ethical practice can be improved.

Professional Development and Training

Ongoing professional development is essential for maintaining and enhancing ethical awareness and competencies. Workshops, seminars, and courses on topics such as cultural competency, bias reduction, and ethical decision-making in education can provide educators with the tools and knowledge necessary to navigate the ethical challenges of their profession.

Mentorship and Collaboration

Mentorship is another powerful tool for ethical development. Experienced mentors can offer guidance, support, and a model of ethical behavior in educational settings. Collaborative relationships with peers also provide opportunities to discuss ethical issues, share experiences, and develop best practices that uphold ethical standards.

Self-Care and Personal Growth

Educators' ability to maintain high ethical standards is also linked to their well-being. Engaging in self-care practices and personal growth activities helps prevent burnout and ensures that educators remain effective and committed to ethical teaching. Activities such as mindfulness, exercise, hobbies, and balanced work-life integration contribute to overall well-being and ethical resilience.

Creating an Ethical School Culture

Finally, educators can contribute to the ethical development of their entire school by helping to foster a school culture that values ethical behavior. This can be achieved by participating in school governance, advocating for ethical policies and practices, and leading by example.

The ethical development of educators is a continuous process that significantly impacts the quality of education and the ethical culture of educational institutions. Through regular reflection, engagement with moral philosophy, professional development, and attention to personal well-being, educators can uphold and model the ethical standards necessary for fostering an environment of respect, fairness, and deep learning. These efforts not only enhance educators' professional lives but also serve as a foundation for their students' moral and intellectual growth.

ϷϷϷ

"The integrity of an educational institution is
measured not by its accolades but by the ethical
stature of its students and educators."

ᐁᐁᐁ

TWENTY-ONE
SUMMARY

The essential task of educating is not just to impart knowledge but to mold character, instilling ethical values that students will carry throughout their lives. This book has traversed a wide landscape of ethical issues in education, offering educators a comprehensive guide on how to navigate these challenges thoughtfully and effectively. Each chapter has addressed a different facet of ethical teaching and learning, together providing a robust framework for educators who aspire to foster an environment of integrity, fairness, and respect in their classrooms and beyond.

Foundations of Ethical Education

The book begins by laying the foundational principles of ethical education, emphasizing the importance of core values such as honesty, respect, fairness, responsibility, and compassion. These values are not only pivotal in shaping the moral framework within which students learn but also critical in guiding educators' behaviors and interactions. Establishing a strong ethical foundation helps educators model positive behavior and set a powerful example for students.

Cultivating Integrity and Trust

Key to effective teaching is the cultivation of integrity in the classroom, ensuring that educators themselves practice what they preach. The text highlights how transparency in teaching methods and assessments can build trust, an essential element in the educational relationship that encourages open communication and enhances student engagement. Trust is reinforced by consistency and fairness in handling academic work and behavior, fostering a secure and conducive learning environment.

Promoting Inclusion and Equity

Equity and inclusion are emphasized as critical elements that ensure all students have access to the same opportunities for success, regardless of their backgrounds. This involves creating inclusive curricula that reflect diverse perspectives and ensuring that teaching methods accommodate all students' learning styles and needs. Addressing equity extends beyond the classroom to involve examining institutional policies and practices that might inadvertently perpetuate disparities.

Navigating the Digital Landscape

As technology becomes increasingly integral to education, the book addresses the ethical considerations that arise with its use, from ensuring digital equity to protecting students' privacy. Educators are urged to employ technology in ways that enhance learning while being mindful of the potential pitfalls associated with data security and the digital divide.

Encouraging Critical Thinking and Ethical Reflection

The development of students' critical thinking is paired with ethical reflection, encouraging educators to integrate ethical dilemmas into the curriculum to enhance students' ability to analyze and navigate complex moral situations. This not only aids intellectual growth but also prepares students to face real-world challenges with ethical competence.

Handling Challenges and Supporting Growth

The text also explores the challenges educators face, such as academic dishonesty and the need for maintaining professionalism in digital communications. Strategies for handling these challenges are discussed, emphasizing the importance of creating supportive environments that encourage ethical behavior and academic integrity.

Fostering Professional and Personal Growth

The book underscores the importance of continuous professional development in ethics for educators, advocating for ongoing learning, reflection, and improvement in teaching practices. This professional growth is seen as parallel to personal growth, where educators are encouraged to maintain their well-being as a critical aspect of being able to uphold ethical standards.

Institutional Support and Policy

Lastly, the role of educational institutions in supporting ethical teaching is examined. The text calls for leadership that actively promotes ethical standards and for policies that support educators in implementing ethical practices. This institutional backing is crucial for sustaining a culture of ethics that permeates all levels of education.

In summary, this book provides a thorough exploration of the multifaceted aspects of ethics in education. It offers educators practical guidance on how to integrate ethical considerations into their daily practices and decisions, with the ultimate goal of enhancing both educational outcomes and the moral development of students. By fostering environments that emphasize ethical behavior and decision-making, educators not only enhance their students' academic and personal growth but also contribute to the cultivation of a more just and ethical society.

❦❦❦

Citation And References

This book represents the culmination of extensive research and meticulous analysis, incorporating a diverse range of sources, including numerous books, scholarly studies, and personal experiences. Additionally, I have scoured various websites to gather relevant information and data essential for the compilation of this work. I have taken every precaution to ensure the accuracy of the information presented and have diligently cited all sources to acknowledge their contributions.

Despite these efforts, the possibility of inadvertent errors remains. I deeply value the insights of my readers and appreciate any feedback that can help identify and rectify such inaccuracies. I encourage you to bring any discrepancies to my attention.

Your feedback is not only welcome but crucial, as it will aid in correcting current editions and enhancing the content of future ones. I am committed to maintaining the highest standards of accuracy and reliability in my work and thank you for your support and understanding.

Additionally, I firmly uphold the principle of freedom of speech and expression as guaranteed under Article 19(1)(a) of the Constitution of India, and I respect the diverse viewpoints and expressions of all readers.

ᐅᐅᐅ

Other Books Of The Author

1. Empowering Minds: A Journey into Women's Self-Discovery and Power
2. The Dynamics of Motivation: Catalyzing Thought into Action
3. Meditation and Mental Well Being: The Path to Inner Peace and Clarity
4. The Psychology of Child Education: Nurturing Future Generations
5. Ethical Enlightenment: A Modern Guide to Living with Integrity
6. Voices of Empowerment: Stories of Women Rising Against Odds
7. Social Psychology in Everyday Life: Understanding Human Connections
8. The Essence of Motivational Speaking: Inspiring Change in Others
9. Balancing Acts: Women, Work, and the Will to Lead
10. Guiding with Grace: Raising Children with Compassion and Awareness
11. The Power of Positive Aging: Embracing Life After Fifty
12. Building Resilient Communities: Social Work in Action
13. The Ethical Educator: Principles for Teaching and Learning
14. From Insight to Impact: Social Psychology for a Better World
15. The Ethics of Empathy: A Guide to Ethical Living
16. The Science of Empowering the Self: Navigating Life's Challenges with Psychological Wisdom
17. The Mindful Conscious Leader: Meditation Techniques for Modern Management
18. Pioneering Spirit: Women's Pathways to Leadership and Empowerment
19. Feeling to Healing: The Role of Emotional Intelligence in Child Development
20. Transformative Talks and Words of Inspiration: Insights into Motivational Oratory

❦❦❦

Contact

Dr. Minakshi Bansal
Social Activist
Ahmedabad, Gujarat, Bharat
minakshiindiag20@yahoo.com

❦❦❦

|| LOKAHA SAMASTHAHA SUKHINO BHAVANTU ||

● 131 ●

www.ingramcontent.com/pod-product-compliance
Lightning Source LLC
Chambersburg PA
CBHW020839150726
48196CB00002B/128